CHRISTMAS PROGRAMS
for the Church

Compiled by
Christine Spence

Standard
PUBLISHING
Bringing The Word to Life™

Cincinnati, Ohio

Scripture quotations are taken from the HOLY BIBLE,
NEW INTERNATIONAL VERSION®. NIV®. Copyright © 1973, 1978, 1984 by
International Bible Society. Used by permission of Zondervan.
All rights reserved.

Standard Publishing
Cincinnati, Ohio.
A division of Standex International Corporation
© 2005 by Standard Publishing

ISBN 0-7847-1614-5

Contents

A Christmas Night

Time: 45 minutes–1 hour

"The Wise Man" (page 7), "The Innkeeper" (page 9), "Shepherd's Night" (page 11), and "Mary's Letter" (page 13) may all be performed as one longer service. Or each may stand alone and be performed separately. A suggested service outline follows if all four skits are used. You may wish to substitute familiar songs of your own in place of the suggested songs.

Narrator: Isaiah 9:2: "The people walking in darkness have seen a great light; on those living in the land of the shadow of death a light has dawned."

Skit: "The Wise Man"

Song: "O Little Town of Bethlehem"

Narrator: John 1:10: "He was in the world, and though the world was made through him, the world did not recognize him."

Skit: "The Innkeeper"

Song: "Silent Night"

Narrator: John 1:14: "We have seen his glory, the glory of the One and Only, who came from the Father, full of grace and truth."

Skit: "Shepherd's Night"

Song: "O Come, All Ye Faithful"

NARRATOR: Luke 1:38: "'I am the Lord's servant,' Mary answered. 'May it be to me as you have said.'" Luke 2:19: "But Mary treasured up all these things and pondered them in her heart."

Skit: "Mary's Letter"

Song *[to be played or sung solo as spotlight shines on MARY]:* "Mary, Did You Know?"

The Wise Man
by Robin M. Montgomery

Summary: A wise man first sees the star of Bethlehem and wonders at its significance.

Characters:
WISE MAN
SERVANT

Setting: outdoors/palace roof in Bible times

Props: rich robe for wise man, simple robe for servant, scroll

Running Time: 5 minutes

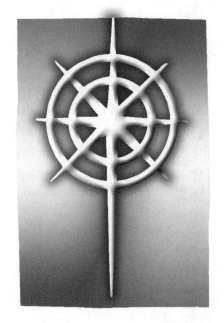

The WISE MAN stands gazing into the sky.

WISE MAN *[to himself]:*
I have studied the stars since I was but a youth—and never before have I seen anything like it. Nowhere in the prophecies of Persia is there mention of a star such as this.

[The SERVANT enters stage with scroll in hand.]

SERVANT: My lord.

WISE MAN *[turns and faces* SERVANT*]:* Have you the scroll?

SERVANT: Yes, my lord. *[hands the scroll to him]* From the writings of the Hebrews, as you requested.

WISE MAN: Thank you. You may go.

*[*SERVANT *bows and exits.]*
*[*WISE MAN *unrolls the scroll and fingers the words.]*

WISE MAN: See how ancient are the words. Perhaps the answer to the star lies somewhere in these Hebrew writings. *[reads from the scroll]* The people living in darkness have seen a great light. On those living in the shadow of death, a light has dawned.

[He looks up, and his gaze is pulled to the heavens.]

WISE MAN: What are you, Great Light, that alters the constellations? Why do you stir my soul like no other star before you? What great moment do you speak of? *[lifts hands to the sky]* Oh, Great God of the Hebrews, show me the meaning of the star.

The Innkeeper
by Robin M. Montgomery

Summary: A busy innkeeper with a full inn sends a young couple to the stable.

Characters:
INNKEEPER'S WIFE
INNKEEPER

Setting: cozy room with a fireplace in a Bethlehem inn

Props: fireplace; bench or mat next to fire for innkeeper's wife; small wooden table and bench for innkeeper; cloth, needle, and thread for innkeeper's wife's sewing; parchment-looking paper and quill for innkeeper's accounts; lamp

Running Time: 5 minutes

The INNKEEPER'S WIFE is seated by the fire quietly working on some sewing. There is the sound of a door closing offstage. The INNKEEPER enters.

INNKEEPER'S WIFE: Someone else wants a room, eh? At this hour, no less.

INNKEEPER *[sets the lamp on the desk, and seats himself to begin tallying again on his very satisfactory accounts]:* Uh-huh.

INNKEEPER'S WIFE: Census stragglers, no doubt. Or worse yet, Roman soldiers!

INNKEEPER: Humph! No, no one *that* important.

INNKEEPER'S WIFE: Ha!

INNKEEPER: Just a young couple from Nazareth. His wife is pregnant. She looks huge! As you did at nine months—remember?

INNKEEPER'S WIFE: I wish I could forget! Such a miserable time I had too. Ah, well, it's too bad they didn't arrive this afternoon. With the rooms being full since supper, we've had to turn away at least a dozen more just this evening.

INNKEEPER: I told them they could use our stable. Unless you think we should give them our bed with her being pregnant and all. . . .

INNKEEPER'S WIFE *[concentrates on picking out a missed stitch]:* I'm sure they won't be too picky at this hour. Besides, it's not as if they're someone *important!* Come now, dear, finish tallying up those accounts. I'm tired!

INNKEEPER: Yes, dear. *[picks up his quill and looks down at his accounts, and then pauses thoughtfully]* So why do I feel as if *I'm* the one missing something? *[shrugs his shoulders and bends his head to his accounts]*

Shepherd's Night

by Robin M. Montgomery

Summary: Two shepherds discuss their encounter with angels.

Characters:
OBED—a shepherd of Bethlehem
JACOB—a shepherd of Bethlehem

Setting: field outside Bethlehem, immediately following the angels' appearance

Props: simple robes and staffs for the shepherds, sheep [optional]

Running Time: 5 minutes

OBED *[rubbing his eyes]:* Did you just see what I saw?

JACOB *[trembling]:* Angels. Angels everywhere!

OBED: That's what I saw, but I can hardly believe it.

JACOB: I wouldn't believe it either if I hadn't just seen it with my own eyes.

OBED: And heard it too. Such music! *[holds hands up to the sky]* Such beautiful music! I wish it could have gone on forever. . . .

Jacob: And did you hear what the angel said? The Christ child has been born.

Obed *[grabs Jacob by the shoulders and shakes him]:* Do you realize what this means? The Savior—our Messiah—is here! In Bethlehem. Right here! *[paces back and forth]* Didn't the angel say we could find Him wrapped in cloths and lying in a manger?

Jacob: Yes . . . but . . . do you think *we're* supposed to go find Him?

Obed: That's exactly what I mean.

Jacob: But we're just shepherds . . . and He is . . . the Messiah!

Obed *[stops pacing]:* Jacob! We just had an invitation from Heaven! What more do you need? *[shakes head]* Why the angels chose to tell *us,* I have no idea. But if what the angel said is true, then I want to see Him with my own eyes. *[turns as if to go, then pauses, and looks back]* Are you coming?

Jacob: Yes. Yes. You're right, Obed. I'll go with you.

Obed *[shouts and lifts hands in air]:* The Savior has been born!

Jacob: Glory to God in the highest!

[Both shepherds hurry offstage.]

Mary's Letter
by Robin M. Montgomery

Summary: Mary writes a letter
to her cousin Elizabeth, following
the birth of Mary's baby, Jesus.

Characters:
MARY—nonspeaking part
ZECHARIAH—nonspeaking part
ELIZABETH—nonspeaking part
MARY'S VOICE
NARRATOR

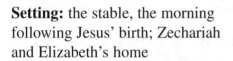

Setting: the stable, the morning
following Jesus' birth; Zechariah
and Elizabeth's home

Props: feeding box with hay, doll wrapped in blanket for baby Jesus,
doll wrapped in blanket for baby John, 2 pieces of parchment for the
letters, a quill for Mary to write with, simple Bible costumes for all
characters

Note: Baby John was about 6 months old at the time of Jesus' birth. If
you have a baby and his parents who could play the parts of Zechariah,
Elizabeth, and John, it would add to the reality of the scene.

Running Time: 5 minutes

*Stage left, MARY is sitting and writing her letter. Jesus is asleep in the
manger nearby.*
*Stage right, ELIZABETH and ZECHARIAH are reading the letter as they
take turns holding baby John.*

The NARRATOR'S voice and MARY'S voice come from the speaker. Spotlight shifts from MARY—as she writes the letter – to ELIZABETH as she reads it.

NARRATOR: History teaches us that Mary, the mother of Jesus, was probably an uneducated girl who couldn't read or write. But if she were able to, how would she describe Jesus' birth in a letter to her cousin Elizabeth?

MARY'S VOICE *[slowly and thoughtfully as though writing the letter as she speaks it]:* Dearest Elizabeth,

My heart overflows with such gladness and joy! I fear that I will burst if I do not write you—you who believed from the beginning. He is here at last!

That first hour, we could not keep our eyes off of Him. Joseph named Him Jesus, just as the angel told him to. And after Joseph had spoken His name, Joseph held our tiny baby in his arms and wept. I heard him whisper, "So this is what God looks like."

Then, even before the morning light began to dawn, shepherds crowded softly around Jesus and began to worship Him! There was awe in their voices as they told of the angel's announcement on the hillside: "Today in the town of David a Savior has been born to you; he is Christ the Lord [Luke 2:11]." They told how the sky burst into song as a great company of angels sang glory to God! Then, as quickly as they came, they left—not returning to their flocks, but to tell others! Oh, Elizabeth, I cannot even begin to describe the joy that filled my heart as I heard the shepherds repeat the angel's announcement. They echoed the angel's promise to me, "He will be great and will be called the Son of the Most High. The Lord God will give him the throne of his father David, and he will reign over the house of Jacob forever. His kingdom will never end [Luke 1:32, 33]." Such a promise! When I look at Jesus, wrapped in nothing but simple cloths, laid in a crude manger, that promise seems impossible—but I know that with our God, nothing is impossible!

I try to imagine what Jesus' life will be like. I see His tiny eyes half closed and I wonder—when He looks at the world around Him, the sea, the sky, the land—will He remember creating it all? Will He look at people and see right into their hearts? I hold His little feet in the palm of my hand—feet so much like any other baby's—yet I am awed by the thought that these feet have walked the very streets of Heaven. How long until they are covered with the dust of this earth? Where will they take Him? His hands are so tiny—yet how strong is His grip! Will they hold a carpenter's hammer and chisel, like Joseph's hands? How many lives will be healed through His touch? And His heart, His tiny heart that has beat since before time began—how many times will it be broken over the mess we have made of our world?

I do not know. Perhaps it is best that way. All I know is that His promises are true. "A Savior has been born. . . ." And He is right here among us!

Praise His Mighty Name, for He has made the impossible possible!

I am the Lord's servant,
Mary

The Treasure of Christmas
by Terri Hutchinson

Summary: This narration can be used for a Christmas Eve Service or any Christmas-themed family service. The purpose of *The Treasure of Christmas* is to make known to children the different names of Jesus, to share the definition of those names, and to illustrate the importance of those names.

Props: large chest to serve as the "Treasure Chest"; small toy crib; silk/plastic grapevine; battery-operated candle; stuffed lion; stuffed toy lamb, preferably one that is well worn and dirty; shepherd's staff (large plastic candy cane wrapped in brown packing tape); gold crown with jewels on it; necklace with a cross made from three nails (available at a Christian bookstore); battery-operated tree-topper star; fishing line; cloth or poster board banners with each name of Jesus— Immanuel, Vine, Light of the World, Lion of Judah, Lamb of God, Good Shepherd, King of Kings, Savior, Bright Morning Star; 9 candles with stands; candle lighter

Running Time: 30–40 minutes

Instructions: Hang the nine banners behind you on the stage. (You could have the children make these in their classes the weeks before your program.) Place an unlit candle in front of each banner. Fill your treasure chest with the items you collected, placing them in order so that the crib comes out first, the grapevine second, etc. Tie the tree-topper star to the fishing line and make a large loop of line. Put one end of the loop around something above the stage. Put the bottom end of the loop around something in your treasure chest or behind your treasure chest so that the star is hidden. When it is time to reveal the star, pull on the fishing line loop to cause the star to rise above the stage.

The songs are suggestions. Include familiar songs for your children and families.

Sit near the front of the stage with your treasure chest beside you. The lights should illuminate you and the banners behind you.

Hello, everyone! Tonight is Christmas Eve. It's my favorite night of the year, and it's so nice to share this time with you.

My name is (your name), and I'm going to share with you the things I consider to be the Treasure of Christmas.

Now I suppose you're wondering why this big chest is up here on the stage. I would like to invite all the boys and girls to come up to sit in front of me, and I will show you. *(Allow time for children to get settled.)*

Did you know that I'm a treasure collector? Yes, I am. And this year I have collected the Treasure of Christmas and put it right here in this treasure chest. Why, even this chest is a treasure. As soon as I saw it, I knew it would make a perfect treasure chest, and I was right. That's because I'm very good at finding treasure.

So are you ready to see the Treasure of Christmas? Of course you are. That's why you're here.

BUT! Let me warn you! Treasure is only treasure if you want it to be. These are the things that are treasure to me.

Immanuel/The Crib

The first thing I want to show you is this: It's a beautiful baby crib, and it can hold a tiny baby. Some baby beds can rock back and forth to help a baby go to sleep.

This is treasure to me because it reminds me of baby Jesus.

He didn't have a nice baby bed like this.

He slept in a dirty manger. A manger held food for the cows and donkeys. Jesus' mother put Him in the food, in the manger, so that Jesus would have a place to sleep.

This baby bed reminds me that Jesus was a baby like you and me and He lived on earth.

God sent His Son to live with us; that's why Jesus is called Immanuel.

The word *Immanuel* means "God with Us."

Song: "Away in a Manger"
[Let a child volunteer help you light the candle by the Immanuel banner.]

<u>Vine/Grapevine</u>

The next item in this chest reminds me of a story.

One day I was walking in the woods with my two friends, and we saw this long rope like thing hanging from the trees. My friend grabbed it and pulled, but it wouldn't come down. She pulled again, and it still would not budge. With the rope still in her hand, she backed way up, and before I knew it, she said, "Here I go," and she swung all the way across the creek. Do you know what she used to swing across the creek? It was a vine.

Can you guess what my next treasure is? It's a vine.

But this is a different kind of vine. Did you know that grapes grow on vines like this?

I love this piece of treasure because Jesus called himself the vine. Jesus said He is the vine and we are the branches.

The branches are connected to the vine, and we need to be connected to Jesus.

This definitely reminds me of Jesus.

[Have a volunteer help light the candle by the Vine banner.]

Light of the World/
Battery-Operated Candle

Now you guys are pretty smart. You are probably starting to figure out that each piece of my treasure is something that reminds me of Jesus.

So let's see if you can guess my next treasure piece. Just please raise your hand if you know the answer.

It can be tiny and small or very big. It can be very bright. It can come from the moon or the sun or even a match.

Let's see if you're right. And of course, it's light.

This candle helps me to see and find my way in the dark. It's really neat because I can turn it on and off whenever I like. *[demonstrate]*

And when it's on, it reminds me that Jesus is the Light of the World.

Song: "O Little Town of Bethlehem"
[Have a volunteer help you light the candle by the Light of the World banner.]

Lion of Judah/Stuffed Lion

I really think you're going to like this next item of treasure. But first, I have to tell you something. Way back in ancient times, a lion was the symbol of the kings and royal families.

These royal families would have a picture of a lion on their fancy robes or on their crowns. Royal families always had kings and queens.

When Jesus was born, He was born to a royal family, a family of kings—they were called the tribe of Judah. The Bible calls Jesus the Lion of Judah. The lion can be a scary animal, but Jesus is not scary.

Jesus is called the Lion of Judah because He's our friend and our Lord.

[Have a volunteer help you light the candle by the Lion of Judah banner.]

Lamb of God/Stuffed Lamb

My next treasure is very, very special to me. It's soft and cuddly and woolly too. It's a lamb. It's a very old lamb, and she's missing some of her fur and her face is a little dirty.

I bet you're probably thinking, "How can that old and worn lamb be treasure? Isn't treasure supposed to be gold and shiny?" Remember what I told you in the beginning: treasure is only treasure if you want it to be. It doesn't matter to me that my lamb is old and a little dirty. Because I love my lamb, it's perfect just the way it is.

This little lamb reminds me of Jesus. Jesus is called the Lamb of God because He's God's Son and because He is perfect.

Song: "Silent Night"
[Have a volunteer help you light the candle by the Lamb of God banner.]

Good Shepherd/Shepherd's Staff

If you wander around in a field all day watching and taking care of about 50 lambs, what would you be called? That's right, you would be a shepherd.

What was the one thing that a shepherd always carried with him? Yes, a shepherd's staff.

The funny thing about lambs is that they can get into quite a bit of trouble. That's the whole reason the shepherd has to look out for them.

Sometimes the sheep and lambs get caught in a thorny bush. The thorny bush holds onto their woolly fur and the lamb gets stuck. The shepherd uses a staff like this to pull the lamb free. *[Demonstrate with your stuffed lamb and your staff.]* Shepherds take good care of their lambs.

This shepherd's staff reminds me that Jesus is called the Good Shepherd because He really, really cares for us. He cares for you and you and you. *[Point to several children.]*

[Have a volunteer help you light the candle by the Good Shepherd banner.]

King of Kings/Gold Crown

When I was a little girl, I used to dream about being a princess. I imagined that I had the most beautiful dress in the whole world and I would live in a great big house with as many animals as possible because if I were a princess, I could have as many animals as I wanted.

I used to dream I had the most beautiful crown made of pink and white flowers. And I wore my crown wherever I went so that everyone would know I was a princess.

Can you guess what my next piece of treasure is? I've given you a hint from my story. It's something a king wears on his head. Of course, it's a crown. The crown is a symbol of distinction and power. A crown is worn by the one who rules the people.

Whenever I look at this crown, I remember that Jesus is called the King of Kings. Jesus rules from above over all things in Heaven and on earth.

Song: "O Come, Let Us Adore Him"
[Have a volunteer help you light the candle by the King of Kings banner.]

Savior/Cross Necklace

Sometimes grown-ups do silly things like lock their keys in their cars or they lock themselves out of their houses. Not that I would know anything about that, but I've heard that people do these things. Anyway, when people can't get into their cars or houses, they have to call someone to rescue them, to help them.

My next piece of treasure reminds me that Jesus is my rescuer, my Savior. This is a necklace that I have.

It's three nails made into a cross, and it's attached to a leather strap.

This is treasure to me, because it helps me remember that Jesus loves me, He rescues me, and He will help me because He's my Savior.

[Have a volunteer help you light the candle by the Savior banner.]

Bright Morning Star/Lighted Star

We have quite a bit of treasure here, don't we? And each piece of treasure reminds me of Jesus. And, guess what, we've learned that Jesus is called by many names. We have one more name—one more piece of treasure left in this treasure chest. I think this next treasure is going to be your most favorite of all that I've shown you so far.

When Jesus was to be born, a star brightly shined in the sky over Bethlehem. Stars do more than just shine in the dark. Stars are like a map that God placed in the sky. A long time ago sailors used the stars to help them find their way as they sailed from water to land.

I love to look up at the sky, because the stars look like millions of diamonds.

But the best thing about the star is that it's a symbol of direction and hope.

The Bible calls Jesus the Bright Morning Star because He is our hope.

Now let's see if I can get a beautiful star to come out of the treasure chest and rise into the sky. *[Flip the switch to light up your star, and pull the fishing line so that it rises in the air.]*

Song: "Joy to the World"
[Have a volunteer help you light the candle by the Bright Morning Star banner.]

The Search for Christmas

by Carol S. Redd

Summary: Two women search for Christmas in very different places.

Characters:
CAITLIN—a woman who is shopping, wrapping, and decorating in her search for Christmas
VAL—a woman who finds Christmas at the local nativity scene; also a vocalist
MARY—nonspeaking part, part of nativity scene
JOSEPH—nonspeaking part, part of nativity scene
JESUS—nonspeaking part; part of nativity scene; a doll wrapped in a blanket could be used

Setting: on a city street, beside a community or church nativity scene

Props: Bible costumes for Mary and Joseph; manger and hay for stable; Christmas outfit with bells for Caitlin; full shopping bags

Running Time: 10 minutes

[MARY, JOSEPH, and JESUS are stage left. VAL enters stage right. CAITLIN loudly sings "Jingle Bells" as she enters down the center aisle dressed in a Christmas outfit that jingles as she walks and carries several full shopping bags. She sees VAL at the front and calls to her.]

CAITLIN: Val! How are you? It's been so long!

VAL: Caitlin? Is that you? . . . I don't think I've seen you since Jackie's party. . . . That was almost two years ago. And look at you! You look like . . . like . . .

CAITLIN: Christmas?

VAL: Well, yeah, . . . I guess. . . . How come you look like that?

CAITLIN: It's because I'm on a Christmas mission.

VAL: A Christmas mission?

CAITLIN: That's right. . . . I'm meeting up with some friends, and we're going out to "search for Christmas."

VAL: Search for Christmas?

CAITLIN: Right. . . . We're going to shop. . . . Well, *[indicating her bags]* shop some MORE. We're going to eat (a LOT), and then we're going back to my house to put up my Christmas tree and wrap packages. If we don't have the Christmas spirit by the time this night is over, I don't think we'll EVER have it. Hey, . . . why don't you go with us?

[VAL is busy looking at the nativity and doesn't respond.]

CAITLIN: Hello! Val?

VAL: Oh, I'm sorry. . . . What did you say?

CAITLIN: I was just saying that my friends and I are going out to "find" Christmas. . . . Do you want to go with us? Val? Hello! Val, . . . what are you looking at?

VAL: Oh, . . . sorry. . . . I was just looking at that . . . what's going on over there . . . where those people are. . . . See them?

CAITLIN: Oh, that. . . . It's nothing.

VAL: Nothing?

CAITLIN: Well, it's just a nativity scene. . . . It's nothing really. They do it every year. . . . No big deal. So what do you say? Want to go with us on our big "Christmas search"?

[VAL continues looking between the nativity and CAITLIN.]

CAITLIN *[continues]:* Come on. . . . It'll be fun. And besides, I even have the car tonight. . . . I'm ready to party. What do you say?

VAL: Well, . . .

CAITLIN: We're going to find Christmas, . . . remember?

VAL: Well *[hesitantly]*, . . . maybe I will.

CAITLIN: Great! Let's go!

VAL: Well, you go on ahead. . . . I'll catch up with you in a minute.

CAITLIN: Fine. . . . I'll go get the car and meet you at the corner. . . . Don't take long though. . . . I want to get started.

[CAITLIN exits down the center aisle. VAL hesitantly and thoughtfully walks to the nativity, sits in front of the manger, and sings "Away in a Manger" or another appropriate song. When the song is finished, CAITLIN reenters down the center aisle.]

CAITLIN: Come on, Val! I'm getting tired of waiting! What's taking you so long?

[VAL gets up from her seat in front of the nativity and walks forward to talk to CAITLIN.]

VAL: You know, Caitlin, . . . I think I'm going to pass on your offer. . . . Maybe we can get together another time.

CAITLIN: But, Val, we were going to "search for Christmas," . . . remember?

VAL: I know. That's OK. . . . You go ahead . . . and, anyway *[looking back at nativity]*, . . . I think I've already found it.

[Bring stage lights down and exit.]

Shopping with Molly

by Margaret Primrose

Summary: A couple discovers the spirit of giving when they take a young girl to the mall to purchase gifts.

Characters:
TERRI DAVIS—organizer of program to provide gifts for children in need
DON MILLER—slightly goofy guy, sponsor of Molly
SUSAN MILLER—Don's wife and sponsor of Molly
MOLLY—an 8-year-old girl
NARRATOR—speaks one line at the end of the skit

Setting: Scene One—church office; Scene Two—bench in a mall

Props: Scene One—desk and 3 chairs for church office; index card and pen; Scene Two—bench; bag of chocolate chip cookies; shopping bag with gifts: a teddy bear, Barbie of Swan Lake® doll (or another popular doll), a CD of a Christian group your kids like, women's bath and body gift set; gift bags for each gift

Running Time: 15 minutes

SCENE ONE

TERRI is sitting at her desk working when DON and SUSAN MILLER enter.

TERRI: Oh, hi, Don and Susan. You must be here to pick up your shopping partner.

DON: Yes, we are. Sorry we're a few minutes late. The car engine doesn't like this cold weather!

TERRI: Let's see. . . . *[consults a card on her desk]* You'll be taking Molly with you today. She and a few of the other kids are playing in the children's church room while they wait. Do you know Molly?

SUSAN: No, not yet. But our daughter goes to school with her brother John, so we know a little bit about her family.

TERRI: Yes. *[consults her card]* She has a baby brother, Micah, a younger sister, Alana, and her older brother is John. Their mom works so hard to keep things together. This will be a great treat for Molly!

SUSAN: Hey, it's a treat for us. Now that our kids are older, we miss shopping for the younger ones. This will be great fun, won't it, honey? *[She nudges her husband.]*

DON: You're just excited that we're going shopping!

TERRI *[winks at Susan]:* Oh, I can understand that. Now do you two have any other questions?

DON [*looks at his wife for confirmation, and she shakes her head no*]: No, I think we're ready to go.

TERRI: All right, then. I just need you to sign this card so that I know where you're going to shop and approximately how long you'll be gone. We'd like to have your cell phone number too, just in case we need to get ahold of you. And while you fill all that in, I'll go get Molly.

[*TERRI exits. SUSAN works on filling out the card while DON paces and rubs his hands nervously.*]

DON: Well, this'll be a first for us. I sure hope we know what we're doing!

SUSAN: Don't worry, dear. I've got it under control.

[*TERRI returns with MOLLY.*]

TERRI: Molly, this is Don and Susan Miller, who are going to take you Christmas shopping today.

DON [*in a high voice*]: Hi, Molly, I'm Susan. [*MOLLY giggles.*] What? I don't look like a Susan to you?

SUSAN [*good-naturedly smacks her husband's arm*]: Don, stop it! Don't pay any attention to him, Molly. We are very glad to meet you. I hope you're ready to hit the mall!

MOLLY: Yes, I am. Thank you.

SUSAN [holds out her hand to MOLLY who takes it]: Then let's us ladies take off! [over her shoulder to DON] We'll let you tag along too, Don!

DON: What a relief! We'll see you later, Terri. Thanks so much for putting all this together.

TERRI: You're welcome. See you in a while.

[All exit. Lights are cut.]

SCENE TWO

DON, SUSAN, and MOLLY enter. DON is carrying shopping bags full of gifts. The empty gift bags should also be in the shopping bags. SUSAN is holding the bag of chocolate chip cookies. There is a bench in the middle of the stage.

SUSAN: Whew! I'm tired from all this walking. How about you, Molly?

MOLLY: Yes, a little.

SUSAN: Here's a bench. Let's sit down and have a cookie. [SUSAN and MOLLY sit on the bench. DON places the shopping bags on the floor in front of the bench.] Do you like chocolate chip?

MOLLY: They're my favorite!

SUSAN: Mine too! [She hands a cookie to MOLLY and takes one for herself.] Do you want one, Don?

DON: Nope. Those three chili dogs I had earlier will hold me.

SUSAN: Chili dogs over chocolate! What is the world coming to? . . . Hey, Molly, while we're sitting here, why don't we go over the gifts we have, and see what we still need to find?

MOLLY: OK.

[SUSAN and MOLLY continue nibbling on their cookies while DON pulls each gift out of the bags.]

DON: That's a great idea! Let's see what we have here. *[He reaches into the bag and, with a flourish, pulls each item out.]* First, a teddy bear . . . for? *[He looks questioningly at Molly.]*

MOLLY: Baby Micah.

SUSAN: He'll love that, Molly!

[DON sets the teddy on the bench next to MOLLY. If he feels comfortable doing it, he can move the teddy bear around and make it talk— "Yes, he will, Molly!"—and give MOLLY hugs.]

DON: And next, ladies and gentlemen, we have a . . . *[He pulls the doll from the shopping bag and questioningly waves it in front of the ladies.]*

SUSAN and MOLLY *[together]:* Barbie of Swan Lake® doll! *[or whatever doll you have chosen]*

DON *[sets the doll next to the teddy bear]:* I knew that.

MOLLY: That's for Alana.

SUSAN: Your little sister, right? The doll is beautiful—what a great gift-giver you are!

DON: The next item we have is . . . a *[name of group]* CD.

MOLLY: My brother listens to music all the time, so I hope he likes it.

SUSAN: Yep. Our daughter has that CD. John will love their music.

DON: And finally, finally, the last item we have is a . . . a . . . bunch of bath-type lotion stuff.

MOLLY: It smells pretty!

SUSAN: Trust me, Molly, your mom works so hard taking care of you guys. She'll love having some pretty stuff for herself.

DON: Now, Molly, we're missing something really important here! Do you have any idea what it is?

[MOLLY shyly shakes her head no.]

SUSAN: There's nothing here for you! What would you like to have? We could get a doll for you, or a new outfit, or what about a new watch? *[MOLLY shyly shakes her head no each time an item is mentioned.]*

MOLLY: No, thank you. I can't think of anything. I just wanted to get stuff for my family so that I would have presents to give them for Christmas.

DON: Molly, that is great! That's what Christmas is all about. I know it makes you feel so happy to give gifts to your family.

SUSAN: Hey, I know what we can do. Let's get out the gift bags and put your presents in them. That way they'll be all ready for when you get home.

DON: And then there's more shopping to do. You see, Susan and I want to get that happy, giving feeling too. And that means that we want to give something to you!

SUSAN: You know what? I think Jesus is very happy with you, Molly. You've figured out what Christmas is about!

[Lights go out; then NARRATOR reads.]

NARRATOR: "You'll not likely go wrong here if you keep remembering that "The Lord Jesus himself said: 'It is more blessed to give than to receive'" *[Act 20:35, NIV].*

It's Only a Job!
by Carol S. Redd

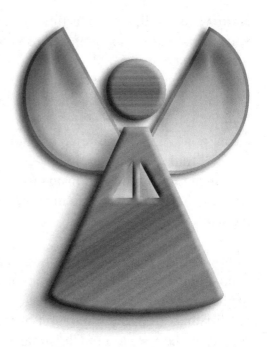

Summary: Two treetop angels discuss the ups and downs of their work in this humorous look at the dark side of our Christmas responsibilities.

Characters:
MELODY—an experienced treetop angel, but ragged around the edges
GABBY—a mall treetop angel with an obvious nervous twitch
JOSEPHINE—new treetop angel who wants to bring "peace on earth"
NARRATOR

Setting: treetop angel break room

Props: Christmas trees with treetop angels on them; cardboard wrapping paper tube; treetop angel costumes—floating, white angel robes, glitter for hair and skin; gummy bears for GABBY'S hair

Running Time: 10 minutes

Note: This skit pokes some lighthearted fun at a staff member and family, so be certain this meets the approval of all who are involved.

NARRATOR: Well, Christmastime is here for another year. How is your Christmas season going? Are you and your family filled with wonder and excitement? Are you anticipating being with family and friends? Have you shared God's love and compassion? Or is this season . . . "only a job" . . . that will be over in a week or so. Hmm. "Only a job." . . . Sounds sad, doesn't it? How did that happen? I mean, none of us ever started out thinking of Christmas as "only a job," . . . did we? No, surely not. . . . There was passion and anticipation and joy welling up inside us until we didn't think we could wait any longer to celebrate the birth of Jesus. But somewhere along the way . . .

This evening *[or morning]* we're going to look at Christmas—not from a human standpoint, but from an angelic standpoint. Oh, not the heavenly ones. But how about, just for fun, of course, we look at Christmas from the standpoint of treetop angels . . . those that are placed on the very top of Christmas trees all over the world. Surely, from their place of honor, as they overlook all that Christmas has to offer, they would never describe Christmas as "only a job" . . . or would they?

[MELODY enters, brushing her robe, straightening her hair, and looking nervously over her shoulder. She is carrying a cardboard wrapping paper tube. A few seconds later, GABBY walks past, occasionally twitching rather violently. She continues twitching occasionally throughout her lines as well as where indicated in the script. She has several gummy bears stuck throughout her hair.]

MELODY: Gabby? Is that you?

GABBY *[hesitantly]:* Yes . . . I'm Gabby. Why? Who are . . . wait a minute . . . Melody? Is that you?

It's Only a Job!

MELODY: Yes. How are you?

GABBY: Oh, I'm *[gives a violent twitch]* fine. I didn't even recognize you. What in the world happened? You look a little . . . um, messed up.

MELODY: Well, Gabby, you know I've been a treetop angel going on 20 years now . . .

GABBY: Me too! I actually just finished my 18th year and, let me tell you, . . . I'm just about ready to hang it up!

MELODY: Tell me about it. I feel the same way. . . . Matter of fact, I think this is my last year as a treetop angel.

GABBY *[obviously twitching]:* Oh, no. Really?

MELODY: What's wrong with you?

GABBY *[a little defensively]:* What do you mean?

MELODY: You've got that twitching thing going on there. . . . What's that all about?

GABBY: Oh *[demonstrating a twitch]*, that! Well, . . . this year I worked on one of the Christmas trees out at the mall.

MELODY: That doesn't sound so bad.

GABBY: Hmmph. You wouldn't think so. Actually, the job wasn't so bad . . . until . . . until . . . *[starts twitching violently]*

MELODY *[pats her consolingly]:* It's OK. . . . It's OK. . . . Just get a grip . . . and tell me what happened.

GABBY: Bubba happened!

MELODY: What?

GABBY: Bubba . . . and he's not a "what"; he's a "who." He's a little kid that came to the mall every day . . . every day . . . and threw gummy bears at me when his mom wasn't looking. *[twitching]*

MELODY: Oh, yeah, I think I see one. *[reaches out and pulls a gummy bear from GABBY'S hair]* Hang on a minute.

GABBY: Ouch! *[grabs her head]* Thanks. Anyway, his mom kept screaming *[in a sicky sweet, grating voice],* "Bubba, where are you?" . . . "Bubba, come over here." . . . "Bubba, you'd better get over here before I count to three." But she never . . . NEVER . . . came to get him. He just stayed . . . second after second *[her voice rises in panic after each statement].* . . minute after minute . . . hour after hour . . . pelting me with those gummy bears. *[frantically looking around]* I think I hear him coming now! *[She tries to hide behind MELODY.]*

MELODY: No, no, Gabby. He's not here. Come on. *[pulls GABBY out from behind her]* You're safe. I promise.

GABBY *[fearfully]:* Are you sure?

MELODY: Positive. *[pats GABBY'S hand]* Now settle down.

GABBY: Whew. OK. Let's talk about something else. *[twitching]* Talking about Bubba makes me crazy, . . . what's that you're holding? *[gestures toward cardboard tube]*

MELODY: Well, it used to be attached to my back, . . . you know, to hold me on the tree.

GABBY: Oh, yeah. How come it's not attached anymore? You poor thing. Did you fall off the tree and break?

MELODY: No. . . . I wish it were that simple, . . . but it's a long story. . . .

GABBY: Well, tell me all about it. . . . The more we talk about you, the less time I have to think about Bubba. *[twitches]*

MELODY: Well, . . . OK. But you have to promise not to tell anyone. . . . It's a really weird little story.

GABBY: OK. . . . I promise.

MELODY: Well, up until last year, I used to work on the trees at the mall too. Then I decided I wanted a more "peaceful" job . . . like being an angel on a nice little tree . . . in a nice little house . . . with a nice little family.

It's Only a Job!

GABBY: Well, that sounds pretty . . . "nice" . . . unless you were assigned to Bubba's family!

MELODY: No. . . . Actually, I was assigned to the *[insert last name of preacher]* family.

GABBY: The *[insert last name of preacher]* family? You mean, the preacher's family?

MELODY: That's right. . . .

GABBY: Well, that is great! *[pause]* Or wasn't it?

MELODY: Oh, I thought it would be great too . . . at first . . . but then it turned out to be . . . very unusual.

GABBY: Unusual? Why?

MELODY: Well, it's just that I thought they would be *[mumbles]*.

GABBY: You thought they would be what?

MELODY: It's just that I thought they would be . . . you know . . .

GABBY: What? You thought they would be what?

MELODY: I thought they would be . . . you know . . . perfect.

GABBY: Perfect?

MELODY: Sure, . . . what with him being the preacher and all . . . and the preacher's wife . . . and the preacher's kids. . . . I just thought they would be . . . perfect.

GABBY: Are you saying they weren't?

MELODY: I'm saying . . . they weren't even close.

GABBY: Not close? Why? What happened?

MELODY: Well, it's just that I was sitting up there on top of their tree . . . minding my own business . . . doing what treetop angels do . . . basically nothing . . . when *[insert name of preacher's wife]* decided that I wasn't sitting quite straight, and I needed to be adjusted.

GABBY: Oh, I hate when that happens.

MELODY: That's not the point. . . . The problem was that she told *[insert preacher's name]* that she couldn't reach me. So she asked him to help her.

GABBY: So? What did he say?

MELODY: He said, "Not now, babe. I'm a little tired. And actually, if you would just fix me a sandwich and a soda, that would be great. Then I think I'll just take a little nap. I'll see if I feel up to helping you fix that angel when I wake up."

GABBY: No!

MELODY: You should have seen the look on her face. . . . It was eerie. . . .

GABBY: What'd she do then?

MELODY: She stomped . . . and I do mean stomped . . . out to the kitchen, . . . slapped together a sandwich, . . . popped the top on a can of soda, . . . stomped back into the living room, and *[insert preacher's name]* was just sitting there staring at the TV. . . . She slammed that stuff down on the coffee table and said, "Don't worry about me, honey. I can fix that angel by myself!"

It's Only a Job!

GABBY: Wow! I didn't think a preacher's wife would ever get mad at her husband.

MELODY: Me neither, . . . but it gets worse.

GABBY: No!

MELODY: Oh, yes. . . . She came back into the living room with a broom and swatted at me on top of the tree, and I went flying across that room and smashed into the wall!

GABBY: Oh, no! Did *[insert preacher's name]* say anything?

MELODY: Well, when I went flying by he yelled, "Get out of my way. I can't see the TV!"

GABBY: Well, no wonder you grabbed that thing *[gesturing to the tube]* and ran out the door!

MELODY: Well, actually, I didn't leave right then, . . . at least not until . . .

GABBY: Until what?

MELODY: Until *[insert preacher's name]* realized he had made a BIG mistake, so he apologized and they got all mushy. . . . Then *[insert name of preacher's wife]* went to get a glue gun to hot glue this thing to my spine! Have you ever had a tube hot glued to your spine?

GABBY: No!

MELODY: Me neither, . . . and I'm not about to either! That's when I ran for the door and ended up here. *[pause]* What in the world is that?

[JOSEPHINE enters down the center aisle from the back of the church.]

GABBY: I have no idea. . . . But look at her. . . . She sure doesn't look like us.

MELODY: Hey, you. . . . Who are you? You're not by any chance a treetop angel, . . . are you?

JOSEPHINE: Oh, no, . . . but that's my dream. I hope that next year I can get a job as a treetop angel and help to spread peace and love all over the world. *[MELODY and GABBY look at each other questioningly and then stare at JOSEPHINE who is very serious.]* I hope that every-one who looks at me will see my gentle loving spirit. *[begins slowly exiting as she finishes talking]* They will love one another, . . . help one another, . . . reach out to one another . . . all because they have been inspired by me and the love I have for the entire world. . . .

[MELODY and GABBY wait until JOSEPHINE is out of sight and then look at each other and burst out laughing.]

MELODY: Well, what was that all about? Peace to the world? *[laughing]* Who does she think she is—Miss Universe? Whew! That's a good one! Obviously, she's never had anything hot glued to her spine!

[MELODY and GABBY exit up the center aisle as they continue talking.]

GABBY: Right. *[sarcastically]* And everybody is going to love each other to death! Yeah, . . . right. . . . That's a hoot! . . . Wait! *[frantic]* I think I hear Bubba! *[twitching]*

MELODY: No, he's not here. I promise. . . . Oh, wait a minute. . . . *[picking from GABBY'S hair]* You've got another gummy bear in your hair.

GABBY: I bet little "Miss Peace to the World" has never been pelted by a giant bag of gummy bears.

MELODY: Right. Little "Miss Everybody Is Just Going to Love One Another" needs to realize that this "Christmas thing" is just another job . . . and nothing else. . . . It's only a job!

GABBY: Exactly! It's only a job!

The Clues to Christmas
by Marla Pereira

Summary: A child travels back in time to discover clues to the true meaning of Christmas.

Characters:
NARRATOR
RYAN—8–10 year-old boy (or girl)
DAD—RYAN's parent (could be Mom)
JONAS—shepherd
SAMUEL—shepherd
MARY
JOSEPH

Running Time: 30 minutes

SCENE ONE

Setting: a child's bedroom with a bookshelf and toys on the floor

Props: lightweight bookshelf, assorted toys and books, toy box, large magnifying glass, watch, small spiral-bound notebook (RYAN's detective notebook), bed (3 chairs, blanket, and pillow), Junior Detective magazine (create or draw a cover and glue it over a child's magazine)

The scene opens in a child's bedroom with toys scattered all over the floor. If needed, you may tape a copy of RYAN's Scene One lines in the Junior Detective magazine to help him remember his lines when he picks up the magazine.

NARRATOR: Our story begins in the little town of Clueless, *[your state]*. With so little time left to prepare for Christmas, a parent finds frustration in trying to get his child to bed.

[Singing jingle bells to himself, DAD walks into the room. He trips on the toy watch.]

DAD *[reaching down to pick up watch]:* What in the world? *[calling out]* Ryan, get in here. Didn't I ask you to clean up your room?

[RYAN comes running in.]

RYAN: Right here, Dad. I was just getting ready to—really!

[RYAN starts picking up the toys and putting them in the toy box while DAD helps. RYAN and DAD should plan to complete picking up the toys by the end of the scene.]

DAD: What is all this stuff anyway?

RYAN: Oh, I'm a Super Dude detective. *[He holds up each item as he mentions it. Then he drops it into the toy box.]* See. This is my fact-finding notebook. A good detective has to take notes. And this is my super spyglass. *[He holds it up to his eye.]* It makes things larger, AND it gives me X-ray vision. And lastly, I have my super time-travel watch. I just used it to take a trip to the year 2050. You should see how cool life is in 2050. *[RYAN holds onto his watch rather than putting it into the toy box.]*

DAD: Well, your time-travel watch worked really well, because it sent me for a trip when I entered your room.

[RYAN sits on his bed with his watch in his hand.]

RYAN: Oh, no. I hope it isn't broken. Oh, man, it was set to 2050, and now it's reading 0000. How am I going to be a Super Dude detective without my super time-travel watch?

DAD: Christmas is coming in two days. You can e-mail Santa for a new super time-travel watch in the morning. For now, please get to bed.

[RYAN lays down on the bed and leafs through his Junior Detective magazine with his lines taped inside.]

RYAN: Dad, David in school said that Jesus wasn't real, just a made-up story. He told me all about the story.

DAD: Well, Ryan, some people don't believe in Jesus. They think Christmas is just for Santa and toys. What exactly did David tell you about the story of Jesus?

RYAN: Let me think. *[pauses, puts his chin on his hand as he thinks]* He said Jesus was a baby king that was supposed to free the slaves from the Romans. And then the Romans knew He was coming because a bright star in the sky told them. But then Caesar got killed by the eyes of March. So they threw Jesus into a lions' den for eating an apple from a private tree that belonged to the Egyptian gods. So then Santa pulled Him out of the lions' den, and that's how we know Santa is a good guy.

DAD *[struggling to hide his amusement]:* Well, I think David has his facts a little confused. Why don't we read the REAL story of Jesus tomorrow?

RYAN *[shrugs]:* OK, I guess.

DAD *[giving RYAN a hug]:* Good night, Ryan.

[DAD leaves room. RYAN stares up at ceiling, thinking.]

RYAN: The thing is, what David said kind of makes sense.
I wonder if all that stuff about a baby king is really real or just
a made-up story.

NARRATOR: Ryan goes to sleep a "little" confused. But during
his sleep, something amazing happens. The time-travel watch
takes him back to the year 0000.

[End of SCENE ONE]

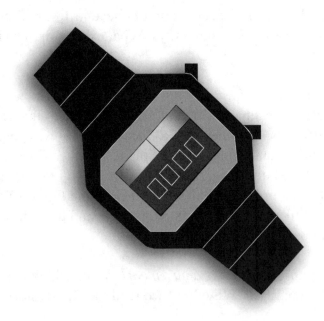

SCENE TWO

Setting: a Bible-times hillside at night

Props: RYAN'S detective notebook, Bible-times costumes and staffs for the shepherds

JONAS and SAMUEL walk onstage mumbling excitedly. They spot RYAN, who is looking around and rubbing his eyes, looking confused.

JONAS *[to SAMUEL]:* Look at this child. He must be from a very distant land. Have you ever seen such strange clothes?

SAMUEL: We should talk to this stranger to see if he is also looking for the new king.

[They cautiously approach RYAN.]

SAMUEL: Young master, we are on a journey to find the baby king that was born this very day. We can tell that you are not from this area. Are you also here to find the king?

RYAN: Noooo. I don't think so. My name is Ryan, and I'm a Super Dude detective. Did you say a baby king? Ooooo. A clue. A clue.

[RYAN flips open his notebook and pretends to write.]

RYAN: So, tell me, what is this king's name?

JONAS *[looks at Samuel and shrugs]:* We don't know.

RYAN: Well, what's he king of?

Samuel: We're not sure, but we were told that He is the Messiah.

Ryan: Ooo. Another clue.

[Ryan quickly scribbles in his notebook and then looks up.]

Ryan: How do you spell *Messiah*?

Jonas: We don't know.

Ryan: You don't know what the king's name is? You don't know what He's king of? You don't even know how to spell *Messiah*? You have no clues or facts. You're not very good detectives, you know. Don't you know you need facts and clues before you believe anything.

Samuel: We're shepherds, not detectives. Besides, we don't even know what a detective is.

Ryan: Why don't you just tell me what you DO know about this king?

Samuel: Well, first of all, stories have been told and passed down through the years from prophets—men whom God told about the future. God told the prophets that certain events would come to pass, and they have now come to pass. So we know this to be true.

RYAN: OK. That sounds promising. What did the prophets say?

[Ryan prepares to write in his notebook.]

JONAS: Well, Isaiah said that a virgin would give birth to a child, and that child would be a son.

SAMUEL: And Micah said that the ruler of the people of Israel would be born in Bethlehem.

JONAS: And Jeremiah said that a new day would come when God will raise up a king from David's line who will rule wisely. All these things are true about this baby. We believe He is the one we have waited for.

[RYAN looks at the shepherd's skeptically.]

RYAN: Wait a minute. How can you be sure? I mean, how did you even find out about this baby being born?

SAMUEL: An angel came to us and told us that we would find the baby in a manger. And an angel wouldn't lie.

RYAN *[in disbelief]:* An angel told you?

JONAS: We need to get going if we are to find this king. We're sorry to leave you, Super Dude detective.

RYAN: Do you mind if I stay with you and travel to see the baby king?

SAMUEL: You're welcome to join us. But if you don't believe us, why do you want to come with us?

RYAN: A good detective doesn't give up that easily. I want to solve this mystery.

[RYAN and the shepherds exit.]

[End of SCENE TWO]

SCENE THREE

Setting: Stable where Jesus was born

Props: RYAN'S detective notebook; Bible costumes for shepherds, MARY and JOSEPH; manger and stable background; hay for the manger; doll wrapped in clothes for baby Jesus

RYAN, JONAS, and SAMUEL approach the stable quietly. MARY is laying baby Jesus in the manger, and JOSEPH is hovering nearby. JONAS and SAMUEL walk forward and bow before the manger. RYAN hangs back shyly.

MARY: Joseph, look at that stranger over there. I've never seen anyone with such strange clothes.

[JOSEPH walks over to RYAN.]

JOSEPH: You seem lost. May I help you?

RYAN: I'm trying to get a look at your baby?

JOSEPH: Who are you?

RYAN: I'm a Super Dude detective. Who are you?

JOSEPH: Well, I'm kind of the baby's father.

RYAN: What do you mean, "kind of the baby's father"? Either you are, or you aren't.

JOSEPH: I know this is going to sound crazy, but actually God is his real father.

RYAN: What? How do you know that?

JOSEPH: An angel came and told me so. An angel also came and talked to Mary to tell her this is God's Son. This is God's child, and I must do my part in raising Him.

RYAN: Not this angel stuff again. I'm not sure there is even such a thing as angels.

JOSEPH: Listen, I'll take you to Mary. Talk to her; then maybe you'll understand.

[JOSEPH leads RYAN over to MARY.]

RYAN: Hi. I'm Super Dude detective, and I'm here to solve the case of the baby king. Tell me, Mary, weren't you scared when an angel came and talked to you?

MARY: At first I was troubled. But then the angel said, "Do not fear, Mary, for you have found favor with God." Then I knew everything would be all right because it was all in God's plan.

RYAN: You people and your angels. How come I never see angels? Are you sure you aren't just making this all up?

MARY: This baby has a lot of work to do for His father in His world. Just look at His face, and you will see.

["Silent Night" plays in the background as RYAN looks at baby Jesus.]

NARRATOR: As Ryan looked into the eyes of the baby, it all became clear to him. He felt a feeling of truth and pure love that he had never felt before. He knew at that moment that there was no deception. This baby was destined to be a king like no other.

[End of SCENE THREE]

The Clues to Christmas

SCENE FOUR

Setting: RYAN'S bedroom, the following morning. RYAN'S spy gear is scattered on the floor.

Props: Same as Scene One.

DAD enters and trips again over RYAN'S time-travel watch.

DAD: Good morning, bud. Hey, didn't we clean this room last night? What did you do—stay up playing all night?

RYAN *[looking confused]:* No, I wasn't up. I don't know how that stuff got there.

[RYAN jumps out of bed and picks up his notebook. He opens it up and his mouth falls open.]

DAD: Come on. Let's get this mess cleaned up so that we can get some breakfast!

RYAN *[stuttering]:* B-b-but! Look, Dad! My notes! They're here. It wasn't a dream?

DAD: Uh, Ryan, what are you talking about?

RYAN: The baby king—Jesus. He's real. I mean, He was real. I mean, He is real. I'm so confused. No, wait! I'm not confused. I think I get it. Yes, I really get it now.

DAD: Good! Because now I think I'm confused.

RYAN: I've solved the mystery, Dad. I know the truth now—the truth about the baby king. Christmas isn't really about Santa. You see, Micah wrote about how He would be born in Bethlehem. And we know it's true because the angels told the shepherds. There were so many clues!

DAD: Wow, Ryan. Those are some pretty important clues about Jesus' birth. I do think you are on your way to becoming a SUPER Super Dude detective. Come on, detective, let's go get some food!

[DAD heads out the door.]

RYAN: Thanks, Dad. I'm coming. *[RYAN looks down at his watch and then over to the place where the stable was.]* And thank You, Jesus— the baby king.

[End of SCENE FOUR]

A Display of Thanks

Summary: A program designed to help families focus on their thanks to God.

Materials: For each family, provide a poster board, markers, items and directions for Thanksgiving turkey cookies (see recipe), a Bible, a large candle, and a lighter. For the group, provide a CD of thankful songs.

Option: If you have access to a digital camera and a projector or computer screen, take pictures of families as they arrive and throughout their activity time. Set up a slide show on your screen or computer, so that families can see themselves giving thanks.

Set up so that each family can sit together around a table. Print a "thankful" Scripture reference on each poster board: 1 Chronicles 16:8; Psalm 7:17; Psalm 30:12; Psalm 95:2; Psalm 100:4; Psalm 107:1; Psalm 118:28; Psalm 136:1; 1 Thessalonians 5:18.

Place a Bible and ingredients for assembling Thanksgiving Turkey cookies at each table. Also place a large candle in the center of each table.

As families arrive, direct them to a table. Ask them to find the Scripture reference in the Bible and read it as a family. They can work together to print the words to the verse on the poster and then add pictures or words of things they thank God for.

When they are done with their posters, let families take turns reading their Scripture verses and sharing things they are thankful for. Then sing some family-friendly songs of thanks to God.

Finally, allow families an opportunity to share their thankful hearts with others. Ask them to work together to decorate Thanksgiving Turkey cookies. They can make enough cookies for themselves and for others. As a family, they will choose someone to share their cookies with.

Close with a prayer of thanks to God. Have a leader call out thankful phrases. After each phrase, the entire group should enthusiastically say, "Give thanks to the Lord!"

THANKSGIVING TURKEY COOKIES

Oatmeal cookies
Small (bite-sized) Reese's® peanut butter cups
Chocolate chips
Red string licorice
Chocolate frosting
Candy corn
Plastic knives for decorating

Use frosting to attach decorations to the cookie. The Reese's® cup will be the turkey's body. Attach a chocolate chip to the top of the Reese's cup to be the turkey's head and a little strip of red licorice to be his gobbler. Use frosting to place candy corn in a semicircle on the cookie around the Reese's cup to make the turkey's feathers.